Denver Broncos Trivia Quiz Book

500 Questions On All Things Orange

Chris Bradshaw

Front cover image created by headfuzz by grimboid. It's available to buy as a poster. Order it online from:

https://www.etsy.com/uk/shop/headfuzzbygrimboid

Introduction

Think you know about the Denver Broncos? Put your knowledge to the test with this selection of quizzes on all things orange.

The book covers the whole history of the franchise, from its inception in the 1960s, the Orange Crush era of the 1970s, the near misses of the 1980s and the World Championship teams of the 1990s, right up to the Peyton Manning-led resurgence of today.

All the big names are present and correct so look out for questions on the likes of John Elway, Terrell Davis, Shannon Sharpe, Randy Gradishar, Karl Mecklenburg, Von Miller and many, many more.

There are 500 questions in all covering rushers and receivers, coaches and quarterbacks, pass rushers and punters and much else besides.

Each quiz contains a selection of 20 questions and is either a mixed bag of pot luck testers or is centered on a specific category such as the 1990s or running backs. There are easy, medium and hard questions offering something for newbies as well as testing the brain power of the most ardent Broncomaniacs.

You'll find the answers to each quiz below the bottom of the following quiz. So for example, the answers to Quiz 1: John Elway, are underneath Quiz 2: Pot Luck. The only exception are the answers to Quiz 25: Numbers which can be found under the Quiz 1 questions.

We hope you enjoy the Denver Broncos Trivia Quiz Book.

About The Author

Chris Bradshaw lives in Birmingham, England and has been following the Broncos for over 30 years.

In the 1980s when his classmates were writing to the Queen, Margaret Thatcher and Duran Duran for the "send a letter to a famous person school project" he was penning a note to John Elway. The Broncos replied in style and he's been a dedicated fan ever since.

He has written 14 quiz books including titles for Britain's biggest selling daily newspaper, The Sun, as well as for The Times. In addition to the NFL, he has written extensively on soccer, cricket, darts and poker.

Go Broncos!

CONTENTS

Quiz 1: John Elway Part 1

1. Elway famously wore which number jersey?

2. Who was the Broncos head coach during Elway's rookie season?

3. Which team drafted Elway with the first pick of the 1983 NFL draft?

4. Which future coach was Elway's back-up in Denver from 1983 until 1991?

5. Elway played college football at which university?

6. Which form of transport was also the nickname of a famous Elway play in Super Bowl XXXII?

7. Elway threw an 80-yard touchdown pass in Super Bowl XXXIII to which receiver?

8. Elway made his final appearance as a Bronco against which team?

9. True or false – Elway punted seven times in his NFL career?

10. Elway appeared in how many Super Bowls?

11. Which baseball team drafted Elway in the second round of the 1981 MLB draft?

12. Elway's pro career spanned how many seasons?

13. In which state was Elway born?

14. Elway was sacked 516 times in his career which puts him second all-time behind which other quarterback?

15. What is Elway's middle name?

16. Which receiver caught the most touchdown passes thrown by

Elway? 41 in all.

17. Who caught Elway's last touchdown pass as a Bronco?

18. True or false – Elway threw at least 10 interceptions in each year of his pro career?

19. How many touchdown passes did Elway throw in his regular season career? a) 299 b) 300 c) 301

20. How old was Elway when he won his final Super Bowl? a) 37 b) 38 c) 39

Quiz 25: Answers

1. Dan Reeves and John Fox 2. Miami 3. True 4. Washington 5. Wade Phillips 6. Jake Plummer 7. Ronnie Hillman 8. Tyrone Braxton 9. Brandon Lloyd 10. None 11. Cleveland, Kansas City, Miami, New York Jets and San Diego 12. True 13. Detron Smith 14. Tyrone Braxton 15. Tom Jackson 16. 0 17. Dwayne Carswell 18. Mike Lodish 19. b) Two 20. c) 1992

Quiz 2: Pot Luck

1. The Broncos won their first Super Bowl at which stadium?

2. Which Bronco was the first undrafted player to top 10,000 receiving yards?

3. 'Pot Roast' is the nickname of which former Broncos run-stuffer?

4. Which former Bronco hosts a podcast called 'The Stinkin' Truth'?

5. B'Vsean is the middle name of which Broncos defensive star?

6. True or false – Trey Parker and Matt Stone, creators of the TV show 'South Park', are avid Broncos fans?

7. In 2014, Broncos fans started a petition to try and stop which broadcaster from covering Denver games?

8. In 2011, the Broncos beat which divisional rival on the road despite quarterback Tim Tebow completing just two passes?

9. Who rushed for 218 yards and scored a team record five touchdowns against the Chiefs in December 2003?

10. Who led the Broncos in tackles for nine successive seasons in the late 1970s and early 1980s?

11. Which Broncos legend made a cameo appearance in a 1995 episode of the sci-fi TV drama 'Sliders'?

12. With five receptions for 38 yards, who was the Broncos' leading receiver in Super Bowl XXXII?

13. Which wide receiver caught a Denver rookie record 91 passes in 2008?

14. Running back C.J. Anderson attended which college?

15. Which two former Broncos featured in the list of the 'Top 10 Most Feared Tacklers in NFL History' according to NFL Films?

16. Before the Broncos' triumph in 1997, who was the last AFC team to win the Super Bowl?

17. How many touchdown passes did John Elway throw in his five Super Bowl appearances?

18. In 2008, which running back received a surprise call up to the roster despite having spent the previous three months working in a cellphone store?

19. How many regular season wins did John Elway record during his stellar career? a) 138 b) 148 c) 158

20. In what year did Pat Bowlen become the owner of the Broncos? a) 1982 b) 1984 c) 1986

Quiz 1: John Elway Part One Answers

1. Seven 2. Dan Reeves 3. Baltimore Colts 4. Gary Kubiak 5. Stanford 6. The helicopter 7. Rod Smith 8. Atlanta Falcons 9. True 10. Five 11. New York Yankees 12. Sixteen 13. Washington 14. Brett Favre 15. Albert 16. Shannon Sharpe 17. Rod Smith 18. True 19. 300 20. 38

Quiz 3: Terrell Davis

1. How many seasons did Davis play in the NFL?

2. Prior to being drafted by the Broncos, Davis played for which college team?

3. What number did Davis wear for the Broncos?

4. Davis had to sit out the second quarter of Super Bowl XXXII because he was suffering from what?

5. What is Davis' middle name?

6. How many touchdowns did Davis score in Super Bowl XXXII?

7. How many yards did he rush for in that game?

8. In which round did the Broncos select Davis in the 1995 NFL draft?

9. In eight play off appearances, Davis rushed for over 100 yards how many times?

10. Davis broke the 2000-yard rushing barrier in the final game of the 1998 regular season. Against which team?

11. In 1998, Davis ran for a touchdown in how many consecutive games?

12. Davis ran for a career-best 215 yards and a touchdown in September 1997 against which team?

13. In which city was Davis born?

14. Davis started his college football career with which small, California school?

15. True or false – Davis was a guest on children's TV show 'Sesame

Street'?

16. Davis first rose to prominence as a Bronco after a crushing special teams hit in a preseason game against which team?

17. In which overseas capital city did that preseason game take place?

18. Davis' longest run from scrimmage was a 71-yard scamper in 1996 against which AFC rival?

19. How many yards did Davis rush for during the 1998 regular season? a) 2006 b) 2007 c) 2008

20. How many touchdowns did Davis score during that record-breaking regular season? a) 19 b) 21 c) 23

Quiz 2: Answers

1. Qualcomm Stadium, San Diego 2. Rod Smith 3. Terrance Knighton 4. Mark Schlereth 5. Von Miller 6. True 7. Phil Simms 8. Kansas City 9. Clinton Portis 10. Randy Gradishar 11. Tom Jackson 12. Shannon Sharpe 13. Eddie Royal 14. Cal 15. John Lynch and Steve Atwater 16. LA Raiders in 1983 17. Three 18. Tatum Bell 19. b) 148 20. b) 1984

Quiz 4: Pot Luck

1. 'Through My Eyes' was the title of the best-selling 2011 autobiography by which former Bronco?

2. What is the highest number of losses endured by the Broncos in a single season?

3. Which quarterback did the Broncos acquire in the trade that saw Jay Cutler join the Chicago Bears?

4. Prior to Tim Tebow, who was the last Heisman Trophy winner to play for the Broncos?

5. In 2008, which running back led the Broncos in rushing with just 343 yards?

6. Which Oakland Raiders quarterback threw a record seven interceptions against the Broncos in October 1977?

7. Up to the end of the 2014 season, Denver had a losing regular season record against which six AFC franchises?

8. Who was the first Bronco to catch over 100 regular season passes three times?

9. True or false – only one wide receiver caught a pass for the Broncos in their Super Bowl XXXII triumph?

10. Which running back, whose first name and surname start with the same letter, led the Broncos in rushing in 1991 and 1992?

11. Which Bronco caused outrage in 1997 after spitting in the face of San Francisco's J.J. Stokes?

12. The Broncos set the record for the fastest win in NFL overtime history with a stunning 2012 playoff victory over which team?

13. Who were the two back up quarterbacks on the Broncos' Super Bowl XXXII roster?

14. Brock Osweiler's first touchdown pass as a Bronco was caught by which receiver?

15. Since 1980, only two of the Broncos' first round draft picks have a first name and surname that starts with the same letter. Which two?

16. 'The Human Plow' was the nickname of which highly successful Broncos full back?

17. Running back Ronnie Hillman played college ball at which school?

18. Prior to Demaryius Thomas in 2010, who was the last wide receiver drafted by the Broncos in the first round?

19. Throughout his regular season career, John Elway passed for how many yards? a) 51,475 b) 52,475 c) 53,475

20. What is the capacity of Sports Authority Field at Mile High? a) 71,625 b) 75,621 c) 76,125

Quiz 3: Terrell Davis Answers

1. Seven 2. Georgia Bulldogs 3. 30 4. a migraine 5. Lamar 6. Three 7. 157 8. 6th 9. Seven 10. Seattle Seahawks 11. Eight 12. Cincinnati Bengals 13. San Diego 14. Long Beach State 15. True 16. San Francisco 49ers 17. Tokyo 18. Baltimore Ravens 19. 2008 20. 23 (21 rushing and 2 receiving)

Quiz 5: Receivers

1. Who set the Broncos regular season record of 1,619 receiving yards in 2014?

2. Who caught 101 passes in his first season as a Bronco in 2014?

3. Who is the Broncos' all-time leading receiver in yards?

4. Which former Bronco set the record for the most catches in a single game against Indianapolis in 2009?

5. How many catches did the receiver make to set the record in question four?

6. Which former Bronco is married to country singer Jessie James?

7. Which receiver caught the touchdown pass that took the 1987 AFC Championship game to overtime?

8. Which Broncos tight end caught 396 passes for 5,755 yards including 41 touchdowns between 1972 and 1983?

9. Which former Broncos receiver spent four seasons playing college basketball for Portland State?

10. With 113 regular season grabs, who holds the record for the most catches by a Bronco in a season?

11. Which tight end caught his first touchdown pass in his fourth season with the Broncos in the 47-17 blowout of the Raiders in December 2014?

12. Which Bronco holds the record for the most catches in a single Super Bowl?

13. In the 2014 regular season, which Bronco caught 43 passes, 12 of which were for touchdowns?

14. Which undrafted free agent caught 353 passes for 6,112 yards in a nine-year career with the Broncos that stretched from 1979 until 1987?

15. Prior to joining the Broncos, Ed McCaffrey had spells with which two NFC teams?

16. Which Broncos receiver just missed out on qualification for the 1984 US Olympic team in the long jump?

17. Who were the first three receivers to make 500 career catches for the Broncos?

18. Which Broncos receiver was born on Christmas Day, 1987?

19. Tim Tebow threw 17 touchdown passes as a Bronco. Who caught more of them than any other receiver? a) Eric Decker b) Eddie Royal c) Demaryius Thomas

20. What were receivers Vance Johnson, Ricky Nattiel and Mark Jackson collectively known as? a) The Three Amigos b) The Three Wise Men c) The Three Musketeers

Quiz 4: Answers
1. Tim Tebow 2. 12 3. Kyle Orton 4. Ron Dayne 5. Peyton Hillis 6. Ken Stabler 7. Buffalo, Jacksonville, Kansas City, Miami, Oakland and Tennessee 8. Brandon Marshall 9. True – Ed McCaffrey 10. Gaston Green 11. Bill Romanowski 12. Pittsburgh Steelers 13. Bubby Brister and Jeff Lewis 14. Virgil Green 15. Steve Sewell and Tim Tebow 16. Howard Griffith 17. San Diego State 18. Ashley Lelie 19. a) 51,475 20. c) 76,125

Quiz 6: Pot Luck

1. In 2012, the Broncos traded Tim Tebow to which team?

2. Which Pittsburgh Steelers Hall of Fame linebacker was the first man to sack John Elway in an NFL game?

3. True or false – John Elway once made a guest appearance on Sesame Street?

4. Which former Bronco co-wrote the thrillers 'Monday Night Jihad', 'Blown Coverage' and 'Inside Threat'?

5. Which Broncos great was the color co-commentator on Denver game radio broadcasts on 850KOA in 2015?

6. Before Tim Tebow who was the last left-handed quarterback to start for the Broncos?

7. The award-winning book 'Slow Getting Up' was written by which one-time Broncos tight end?

8. Which former Detroit Lion led the Broncos in rushing in 2004 with 1,240 yards?

9. Which Denver O-lineman played every snap of the 2008 season but failed to give up a single sack?

10. Shannon Sharpe spent 12 of his 14 years in the NFL in Denver. The tight end enjoyed a brief but successful stint with which other team?

11. Who were the two starting tackles in the Broncos' first winning Super Bowl appearance?

12. Montee Ball played college ball at which university?

13. In September, which former Bronco became a co-host on the breakfast show on radio station 104.3 The Fan?

14. The Broncos drafted a wide receiver in the first round of the 1998 draft. What was his name?

15. True or false – it's possible to get married at Sports Authority Field at Mile High?

16. Before Terrell Davis, who was the last Bronco to rush for 1,000 yards in a season?

17. Which Denver cornerback was named in the NFL Team of the Decade for the 1970s?

18. Who was the first Bronco in franchise history to rush for over 1,000 yards and catch for over 500 yards in the same season?

19. Which legendary Bronco's first catch as a pro was a last-minute, 43-yard TD against Washington in September 1995? a) Terrell Davis b) Shannon Sharpe c) Rod Smith

20. Which team have the Broncos beaten more often than any other in franchise history? a) Kansas City b) Oakland c) San Diego

Quiz 5: Answers

1. Demaryius Thomas 2. Emmanuel Sanders 3. Rod Smith 4. Brandon Marshall 5. 21 6. Eric Decker 7. Mark Jackson 8. Riley Odoms 9. Julius Thomas 10. Rod Smith 11. Virgil Green 12. Demaryius Thomas 13. Julius Thomas 14. Steve Watson 15. New York Giants and San Francisco 49ers 16. Vance Johnson 17. Lionel Taylor, Shannon Sharpe and Rod Smith 18. Demaryius Thomas 19. Eric Decker 20. The Three Amigos

Quiz 7: Peyton Manning

1. What number jersey does Manning wear?

2. Prior to joining the Broncos, Manning played for which club?

3. True or false – Manning enjoyed a quarterback rating of over 100 in each of his first three season in Denver?

4. Manning played college football at which school?

5. What is the name of Manning's pro football playing father?

6. In 2014, Manning was named the greatest athlete to have come from which state?

7. In October 2013, Manning broke Brett Favre's record of 508 touchdown passes. Who caught the historic pass?

8. In May 2011, Manning famously underwent surgery on which part of his body?

9. In 2014, Manning became the second oldest quarterback to start in a Super Bowl. Who is the oldest?

10. Manning threw his 400th career touchdown pass in his first game as a Bronco. Against which team?

11. Who caught that famous 400th pass?

12. In the fall of 2012, Manning invested in 21 franchises of which fast-food chain?

13. What is Manning's middle name?

14. Manning is one of only two quarterbacks to have recorded victories against all 32 NFL teams. Who is the other?

15. Manning was fined $8,286 by the NFL after being flagged for taunting which Houston Texans linebacker?

16. Manning threw a record seven touchdown passes in the opening game of the 2013 season. Who were the Broncos' opponents?

17. True or false – Manning threw at least 10 interceptions in each of his first three seasons with the Broncos?

18. Manning scampered for a cheeky 1-yard touchdown run during a 2013 shootout against which team?

19. A zoo in Knoxville honored Manning by naming an animal after him. What sort of animal? a) giraffe b) panda c) tiger

20. How many touchdown passes did Manning throw during his record-breaking 2013 season? a) 53 b) 54 c) 55

Quiz 6: Answers

1. New York Jets 2. Jack Lambert 3. False 4. Jason Elam 5. Ed McCaffrey 6. Chris Simms 7. Nate Jackson 8. Reuben Droughns 9. Ryan Clady 10. Baltimore Ravens 11. Gary Zimmerman and Tony Jones 12. Wisconsin 13. Joel Dreesen 14. Marcus Nash 15. Tree 16. Gaston Green 17. Louis Wright 18. Knowshon Moreno 19. Rod Smith 20. San Diego

Quiz 8: Pot Luck

1. Which Bronco was fined $11,567 by the NFL following a particularly raunchy dance after recording a sack against Detroit in September 2015?

2. Who scored the Broncos' only touchdown in Super Bowl XLVIII?

3. Who was the first Broncos running back to have his jersey number retired?

4. Which former Bronco is the owner of a thoroughbred racehorse named Undrafted?

5. True or false – the Broncos' picks in the 2010 draft, Erik Decker and Demaryius Thomas, had the top two scores among wide receivers in that year's Wonderlic test?

6. Which member of the 2015 Broncos roster has the nickname 'Ninja Assassin'?

7. Up to 2015, the Broncos have 100 percent losing records in playoff games against which two AFC rivals?

8. True or false – John Elway attended the same high school as actor Robert Englund who is best known for playing Freddy Krueger in the 'A Nightmare on Elm Street' franchise?

9. @87Ed is the Twitter handle of which former Bronco?

10. Which Broncos running back would celebrate touchdowns with a move known as the 'Mississippi Mud Walk'?

11. Shannon Sharpe played college ball at which southern school?

12. 'Snow Goose' was the nickname of which defensive stalwart?

13. Who was the referee in Super Bowl XXXII?

14. Who rushed for exactly 100 yards in his first career start against the New York Jets in October 2014?

15. Which two defensive players with Broncos connections were named in the 1990s NFL Team of the Decade?

16. True or false – Pro Bowl cornerback Chris Harris Jr was an undrafted free agent?

17. Which running back, who had a brief spell in Denver, spent two years in jail for financing a cocaine trafficking business?

18. Which Broncos offensive lineman played every snap during the record-breaking 2013 season but didn't give up a single sack?

19. Former Broncos offensive lineman Orlando Franklin was born in which country? a) Barbados b) Jamaica c) Trinidad

20. Why is Edwin Guy Taylor an important figure in franchise history? a) he was the first owner b) he made the first snap in Broncos history c) he designed the famous orange D logo

Quiz 7: Peyton Manning Answers

1. 18 2. Indianapolis 3. True 4. Tennessee 5. Archie 6. Louisiana 7. Demaryius Thomas 8. Neck 9. John Elway 10. Pittsburgh Steelers 11. Demaryius Thomas 12. Papa John's 13. Williams 14. Brett Favre 15. DJ Swearinger 16. Baltimore 17. True 18. Dallas 19. a) giraffe 20. c) 55

Quiz 9: Defense

1. Who holds the record for the most career sacks by a Bronco?

2. Who was Denver's defensive coordinator during their first two Super Bowl triumphs?

3. Who recorded 10 sacks in his one and only season with the Broncos in 2013?

4. Who holds the record for the most sacks by a Bronco in a single season?

5. Which member of the Denver Super Bowl winning sides is joint-holder of the record for the most interceptions returned for a TD by a Bronco?

6. Which two defensive backs were selected to play in the Pro Bowl eight times while with the Broncos?

7. Which Broncos DB picked off four passes against Kansas City in July 2001?

8. Which Bronco enjoyed two four sack games during the 1985 season?

9. Who holds the record for the most sacks by a defensive back for the Broncos with 10.5 between 1994 and 2000?

10. Which linebacker never made it to a Pro Bowl but was named First Team All Pro in 1997?

11. Which one-time quarterback holds the record for the most interceptions by a Bronco with 44?

12. Prior to Bradley Roby in 2014, who was the last safety or cornerback

selected in the first round of the draft by the Broncos?

13. Who had more picks for the Broncos – Louis Wright or Champ Bailey?

14. At the start of the 2015 season, which member of the secondary was the Broncos' longest tenured player?

15. Which linebacker holds the record for the most forced fumbles by a Bronco with 20?

16. Kool is the middle name of which former Bronco great?

17. Which Bronco was named NFL Defensive Player of the Year for 1978?

18. Which hard-hitting Broncos safety made the Pro Bowl roster six times between 1985 and 1993?

19. During the Broncos' first Super Bowl winning regular season, three players each recorded 8.5 sacks. Which three?

20. Who intercepted a Brett Favre pass during Super Bowl XXXII?

Quiz 8: Answers

1. Von Miller 2. Demaryius Thomas 3. Floyd Little 4. Wes Welker 5. True 6. Antonio Smith 7. Buffalo and Indianapolis 8. True 9. Ed McCaffrey 10. Sammy Winder 11. Savannah State University 12. Karl Mecklenburg 13. Ed Hochuli 14. Ronnie Hillman 15. Neil Smith and Steve Atwater 16. True 17. Travis Henry 18. Louis Vasquez 19. b) Jamaica 20. He designed the D logo

Quiz 10: Pot Luck

1. 'The Smiling Assassin' was the nickname of which Broncos great?

2. Which former Broncos head coach was in charge of their opponents in Super Bowl XXXIII?

3. By the start of the 2015 season, the Broncos had faced every AFC team in the playoffs bar two. Which two?

4. @Grindin_59 is the Twitter handle of which Broncos defensive star?

5. Which Broncos defensive back was burned for a 70-yard touchdown by Baltimore's Jacoby Jones in the closing stages of the 2013 playoff loss to the Ravens?

6. Hall of Fame tight end Shannon Sharpe was selected in which round of the NFL Draft?

7. The Broncos beat which team 17-14 in a famous 1984 Monday night game when a blizzard blew in for much of the contest?

8. Which position on the roster has been held recently by Lonie Paxton and Aaron Brewer?

9. Former Broncos running back Knowshon Moreno played college ball at which school?

10. Who was the first, and so far only, Broncos receiver to catch four touchdown passes in a game?

11. Which veteran was named AFC Defensive Player of the Month for the first time in September 2015?

12. Who were the four Broncos named in the NFL Offensive Team of the

Decade for the 1990s?

13. Which former Broncos back-up quarterback was named Oakland's offensive coordinator in 2015?

14. Who was the emergency quarterback on Denver's two Super Bowl-winning rosters?

15. Which Broncos back-up quarterback came off the bench to throw two fourth-quarter touchdowns with his only two passes as the Broncos routed Seattle 31-7 on the road in November 2002?

16. The Broncos had two first round picks in the 2009 draft. Which two players did they select?

17. Who led the Broncos in rushing for seven successive seasons from 1967 until 1973?

18. The full names of which two members of the Broncos' Super Bowl XXXIII roster start and end with the same letter?

19. Since the AFL/NFL merger in 1970, what is the longest stretch the Broncos have gone without posting a winning regular season record? a) three seasons b) four seasons c) five seasons

20. In which round of the 1993 NFL Draft did the Broncos select Jason Elam? a) 3rd b) 4th c) 5th

Quiz 9: Answers
1. Simon Fletcher 2. Greg Robinson 3. Shaun Phillips 4. Von Miller 5. Tyrone Braxton 6. Steve Atwater and Champ Bailey 7. Deltha O'Neal 8. Karl Mecklenburg 9. Ray Crockett 10. John Mobley 11. Steve Foley 12. Willie Middlebrooks 13. Champ Bailey 14. David Bruton Jr 15. Simon Fletcher 16. Elvis Dumervil 17. Randy Gradishar 18. Dennis Smith 19. Neil Smith, Alfred Williams and Maa Tanuvasa 20. Tyrone Braxton

Quiz 11: Running Backs

1. With 849 yards, who was Denver's leading rusher in 2014?

2. Who is Denver's all-time leading rusher?

3. Which Bronco rushed for over 1,000 yards in his first two seasons with the Broncos in 1989 and 1990 before being traded to the Miami Dolphins for Sammie Smith?

4. Who holds the record for the most rushing touchdowns by a Bronco?

5. Which former Baltimore Raven led the Broncos in rushing in 2011 and 2012?

6. Who was Denver's leading rusher for five consecutive years between 1983 and 1987?

7. Four Broncos running backs rushed for touchdowns in 2014. Which four?

8. Which running back left for Washington as part of the deal that brought Champ Bailey to Denver?

9. Which Broncos running back had just four carries in Super Bowl XXXIII but rushed for two touchdowns?

10. Who had more rushing yards as a Bronco – John Elway or Clinton Portis?

11. Which Bronco holds the record for the most rushing yards in a game with 251 against New Orleans in 2000?

12. Who are the three Broncos to have rushed for over 5,000 yards?

13. Which member of the Pro Football Hall of Fame spent a single season with the Broncos in 1988?

14. In 2002, the Broncos had four 1,000 yard rushers on the roster. Who were the impressive quartet?

15. Who are the three Denver running backs to have won the NFL rushing title?

16. What do the initials C.J. stand for in C.J. Anderson's name?

17. Which 1980s era Bronco famously celebrated his touchdowns with a back flip?

18. Who had more rushing yards with the Broncos – Mike Anderson or Knowshon Moreno?

19. Of backs with at least 100 carries, which Bronco has the best yards per carry average? a) Mike Anderson b) Terrell Davis c) Clinton Portis

20. Who was the last Broncos running back selected in the first round of the NFL draft? a) C.J. Anderson b) Montee Ball c) Knowshon Moreno

Quiz 10: Answers
1. Steve Atwater 2. Dan Reeves 3. Cincinnati Bengals and Houston Texans 4. Danny Trevathan 5. Rahim Moore 6. Seventh 7. Green Bay 8. Long snapper 9. Georgia 10. Eric Decker 11. DeMarcus Ware 12. John Elway, Terrell Davis, Shannon Sharpe and Gary Zimmerman 13. Bill Musgrave 14. Rod Smith 15. Steve Beuerlein 16. Knowshon Moreno and Robert Ayers 17. Floyd Little 18. Howard Griffith and Harald Hassalbach 19. c) Five seasons – 2007 to 2011 20. 3rd

Quiz 12: Pot Luck

1. Which former Broncos chief was appointed head coach of the Chicago Bears in 2015?

2. 'Stink' is the nickname of which former Bronco turned broadcaster?

3. Who was the only Broncos running back selected to play in the Pro Bowl in the 1980s?

4. Prior to being appointed head coach in Denver, Gary Kubiak was the offensive coordinator at which team?

5. Prior to Von Miller, who was the last linebacker selected by the Broncos in the first round of the draft?

6. Which name comes next on the list and why - Mickey Slaughter, Gary Kroner, Craig Morton...?

7. True or false – Shannon Sharpe was the first tight end in NFL history with 10,000 receiving yards?

8. Since 2000, the Broncos have selected two quarterbacks with first round draft picks. Which two?

9. 'Laying It On the Line' was the title of the 2000 autobiography by which Broncos Super Bowl winner?

10. Shannon Sharpe was famously filmed calling for the National Guard while the Broncos were thrashing which team?

11. Which former Bronco was caught on camera shedding tears during the national anthem prior to a 2013 game against Kansas City?

12. Who were the two starting guards in Denver's Super Bowl XXXII

team?

13. After a lengthy and hugely successful career with the Broncos, Steve Atwater spent a final season with which team?

14. Between 1967 and 1975, only one running back rushed for more yards than Denver's Floyd Little. Which one?

15. Which Bronco set an NFL record in the early 1990s after recording a sack in 10 successive games?

16. The Broncos selected two players from Tennessee with their first round draft picks in 1998 and 1999. Who were the two players?

17. Which quarterback did the Broncos select with the 25th pick of the 1992 NFL draft?

18. Which full back, who is the older brother of an NFL superstar, had a brief spell with the Broncos in 2012?

19. Peyton Manning holds the record for the most consecutive games with a touchdown pass by a Denver quarterback. Whose record did he break? a) Jay Cutler b) Brian Griese c) Jake Plummer

20. How many turnovers did the Broncos give up in Super Bowl XII? a) 6 b) 7 c) 8

Quiz 11: Answers
1. C.J. Anderson 2. Terrell Davis 3. Bobby Humphrey 4. Terrell Davis 5. Willis McGahee 6. Sammy Winder 7. C.J. Anderson, Hillman, Ball, Thompson 8. Clinton Portis 9. Howard Griffith 10. John Elway 11. Mike Anderson 12. Terrell Davis, Floyd Little and Sammy Winder 13. Tony Dorsett 14. Mike Anderson, Reuben Droughns, Olandis Gary, Clinton Portis 15. Davis, Little and Otis Armstrong 16. Cortrelle Javon 17. Gerald Willhite 18. Mike Anderson 19. Clinton Portis 20. Knowshon Moreno

Quiz 13: Special Teams

1. Who is the only player in Broncos history to have returned at least two punts and two kickoffs for touchdowns?

2. The Broncos acquired kicker Brandon McManus via a trade with which team?

3. Which punter holds the record for the best gross average in a single season at 47.4 yards per kick?

4. True or false – John Elway kicked a field goal in a regular season game?

5. Which punter converted his one and only field goal for the Broncos against San Diego in November 2003?

6. Which kicker was cut by the Broncos despite going 15 of 16 on field goal attempts in his short spell with the club?

7. Which running back holds the record for the most kick returns in Broncos history with 134 between 1996 and 1998?

8. Who are the two Broncos punters to have been named First Team All Pros?

9. Who set the NFL record for the longest punt return in postseason history against Baltimore in 2013?

10. Who holds the record for the most punts returned for a touchdown by a Bronco with eight?

11. Jason Elam booted a record-breaking 63-yard field goal in October 1998 against which team?

12. Matt Prater eclipsed Elam's record with a 64-yard effort against which team in December 2013?

13. Who are the four Denver kickers to have been voted to the Pro Bowl?

14. Who holds the record for the most successful field goals in a game for the Broncos with seven?

15. With 641 punts, who has been the most prolific punter in Broncos history?

16. Which Bronco holds the unwanted record of missing the shortest field goal (just 23 yards) in Super Bowl history?

17. Which kicker holds the record for the most points scored by a Bronco in a single season?

18. Which Bronco led the NFL in punt return touchdowns after taking three to the house in 1997?

19. Jason Elam attempted 604 extra points in his time with the Broncos. How many of those kicks did he miss? a) 3 b) 4 c) 5

20. Matt Prater set the record for the most extra points in a single season in 2013. How many PATs did he make? a) 65 b) 70 c) 75

Quiz 12: Answers
1. John Fox 2. Mark Schlereth 3. Sammy Winder 4. Baltimore Ravens 5. DJ Williams 6. John Elway (they wore the number 7 jersey) 7. True 8. Jay Cutler and Tim Tebow 9. Howard Griffith 10. New England Patriots 11. Knowshon Moreno 12. Mark Schlereth and Brian Habib 13. New York Jets 14. OJ Simpson 15. Simon Fletcher 16. Marcus Nash and Al Wilson 17. Tommy Maddox 18. Chris Gronkowski 19. Brian Griese 20. c) 8

Quiz 14: John Elway Part 2

1. How many times did Elway throw for over 4,000 yards in a season?

2. Which receiver caught Elway's longest pass, an 86-yard effort against the Raiders in 1988?

3. With 44 touchdowns passes, Elway was most prolific against which opponent?

4. How many times was Elway voted to the Pro Bowl?

5. Elway's first TD pass as a pro was caught by which running back?

6. Elway graduated from college with a Bachelor's degree in which subject?

7. Who threw the pass that gave Elway his only career receiving touchdown as a Bronco?

8. Which offensive lineman left Denver as part of the package that saw Elway traded to the Broncos?

9. Which quarterback left Denver as part of the same deal?

10. In 1998, Elway became the second player to rush for a touchdown in four Super Bowls. Which running back was the first to manage that feat?

11. Elway tossed a record five touchdown passes in a 1984 game against which team?

12. True or false – Elway never had a single season passer rating of over 100?

13. In what year was Elway inducted into the Pro Football Hall of Fame?

14. Elway enjoyed more career wins against which AFC team than any other?

15. On the opening play of Super Bowl XXII, Elway threw a 56-yard touchdown pass to which receiver?

16. In 1998 Elway became the third QB to throw for 300 TDs. Who were the first two?

17. What was the name of the Arena League franchise in which Elway was a co-owner?

18. True or False – Elway was never named a First Team All Pro?

19. Elway was the architect of how many regular season, fourth quarter comebacks? a) 33 b) 34 c) 35

20. What was the most touchdown passes thrown by Elway in a single regular season? a) 26 b) 27 c) 28

Quiz 13: Answers

1. Trindon Holliday 2. New York Giants 3. Britton Colquitt 4. False 5. Micah Knorr 6. Connor Barth 7. Vaughn Hebron 8. Luke Prestridge and Mike Horan 9. Trindon Holliday 10. Rick Upchurch 11. Jacksonville Jaguars 12. Tennessee Titans 13. Gene Mingo, David Treadwell, Matt Prater and Jason Elam 14. Jason Elam 15. Tom Rouen 16. Rich Karlis 17. Matt Prater 18. Darrien Gordon 19. a) 3 20. c) 75

Quiz 15: Pot Luck

1. Which pass rusher did the Broncos select with their first round pick in the 2015 NFL draft?

2. Who was the Broncos interim head coach after Josh McDaniels was fired in 2010?

3. Which team defeated the Broncos 24-13 in the divisional round of the 2014 play offs?

4. Which former Broncos coordinator was appointed head coach of the Raiders in 2015?

5. Who kicked 56 and 57-yard field goals in the 2015 season opener against Baltimore?

6. Prior to joining the Broncos, cornerback Aqib Talib had played for which two NFL clubs?

7. At what overall position in the draft did the Broncos select Von Miller?

8. By what moniker was Broncos super fan Tim McKernan better known?

9. Which eventual Super Bowl winner defeated the Broncos in the 1998 AFC Championship game?

10. True or false – Robin Williams became the Broncos' first male cheerleader in an episode of the TV comedy 'Mork and Mindy'?

11. The Broncos played their first overseas regular season game in London against which team?

12. Which former Broncos defensive star is the co-host of The Drive on radio station 104.3 The Fan?

13. What number shirt does receiver Emmanuel Sanders wear?

14. How tall is Brock Osweiler?

15. The Broncos drafted which former Colorado State tackle in the second round of the 2015 draft?

16. Which former Broncos linebacker was named the team's offensive coordinator in 2015?

17. Which Hollywood star, who was nominated for a Best Actor Oscar in 2005, is a big Broncos fan?

18. Steve Atwater rose to national prominence after a famous hit on which 260lb Kansas City running back?

19. Between 1976 and 2014, the Broncos suffered how many losing seasons? a) 6 b) 7 c) 8

20. What is the name of the Broncos' mascot? a) Giles b) Miles c) Smiles

Quiz 14: Answers

1. Surprisingly, just once 2. Vance Johnson 3. Seattle Seahawks 4. Nine 5. Rick Parros 6. Economics 7. Steve Sewell 8. Chris Hinton 9. Mark Hermann 10. Thurman Thomas 11. Minnesota Vikings 12. True 13. 2004 14. Kansas City Chiefs 15. Ricky Nattiel 16. Fran Tarkenton and Dan Marino 17. Colorado Crush 18. True 2004 19. c) 35 20. b) 27

Quiz 16: The 1960s

1. In which year did the Broncos make their pro debut?

2. How many games did they win during that first season?

3. True or false – in the 1967 season, the Broncos wore helmets that did not feature a logo?

4. By what nickname was safety Austin Gonsoulin more commonly known?

5. The Broncos won the first ever AFL game. Who were their opponents?

6. What color uniforms did the Broncos wear in their first season in the AFL?

7. True or false – the Broncos were the only team of the original AFL eight who failed to play in a Championship game?

8. 'Tombstone' was the nickname of which Denver defensive lineman who joined the Broncos in 1967?

9. In what year did the Broncos unveil their orange, white and blue uniform?

10. What was the name of the stadium in which the Broncos played home games during their first season?

11. Who was Denver's head coach during their first two seasons?

12. True or false – The Broncos failed to record a winning season throughout the 1960s?

13. Which coach joined the Broncos from the Buffalo Bills in 1967, then

rejoined the Bills in 1972 after five years in Denver?

14. In August 1967, the Broncos became the first AFL team to defeat an NFL opponent when they won a pre-season game against which team?

15. Which future Ring of Fame member started 42 games at quarterback for the Broncos between 1960 and 1963?

16. Which former Chicago linebacker was the Broncos' leading receiver in their first six seasons in the AFL?

17. In 1969, which fleet-footed rookie became the first player to lead the league in both punt and kickoff returns in the same season?

18. The first African-American placekicker to play professional football played for the Broncos. What is his name?

19. What number jersey did All-Pro running back Floyd Little wear? a) 22 b) 33 c) 44

20. How many games did the Broncos win throughout the 1960s? a) 39 b) 45 c) 51

Quiz 15: Answers

1. Shane Ray 2. Eric Studesville 3. Indianapolis Colts 4. Jack Del Rio 5. Brandon McManus 6. Tampa Bay Buccaneers and New England Patriots 7. Second 8. Barrel Man 9. Pittsburgh Steelers 10. True 11. San Francisco 12. Alfred Williams 13. 10 14. 6ft 8in 15. Ty Sambrailo 16. Rick Dennison 17. Don Cheadle 18. Christian Okoye 19. c) 6 20. Miles

Quiz 17: 1970s

1. What was the nickname of the Broncos defense that terrorized opponents in the late 1970s?

2. In 1970, who became the first Bronco to win the AFC rushing title?

3. Which team did the Broncos face in Super Bowl XII?

4. In which stadium did the Broncos make their first Super Bowl appearance?

5. The Broncos made their first appearance on Monday Night Football in a 1973 tie against which rival?

6. Which Bronco made the NFL's All-Decade team for the 1970s as a kick returner?

7. Which team did the Broncos beat in their first ever play off game?

8. And which team did they beat in their first AFC title game?

9. Which Broncos head coach steered Denver to its maiden Super Bowl appearance?

10. Which running back scored the Broncos' only touchdown in Super Bowl XII?

11. Two quarterbacks threw passes for Denver in Super Bowl XII. Craig Morton was one. Who was the other?

12. Which all-time Broncos great was selected with the 14th pick of the 1974 NFL draft?

13. In 1973, the Broncos enjoyed their first winning season. Who was the head coach during that momentous year?

14. Who was the starting quarterback for every game in 1973?

15. Which Broncos running back recorded a single called 'Make Those Miracles Happen' during their first Super Bowl run?

16. Which running back averaged over 100 yards rushing per game during the 1974 season?

17. Which Broncos receiver, who played 140 games between 1972 and 1981, caught five passes for 168 yards and two touchdowns in the 1977 AFC Championship game?

18. Which kicker didn't miss a game in a nine-year career with the Broncos, scoring 742 points in the process?

19. Denver was involved in the NFL's first sudden death overtime game. Who was the opponent? a) Kansas City b) New England c) Pittsburgh

20. In which year did the Broncos make their first play off appearance? a) 1975 b) 1976 c) 1977

Quiz 16: Answers

1. 1960 2. Four 3. True 4. Goose 5. Boston Patriots 6. Light gold jerseys and brown pants 7. True 8. Rich Jackson 9. 1962 10. Bears Stadium 11. Frank Filchock 12. True 13. Lou Saban 14. Detroit Lions 15. Frank Tripucka 16. Lionel Taylor 17. Billy Thompson 18. Gene Mingo 19. c) 44 20. a) 39

Quiz 18: 1980s

1. Appointed by the Broncos in 1981, which 37-year-old became the youngest head coach in the NFL?

2. Which team did the Broncos defeat in three AFC Championship games in the 1980s?

3. Who was the Denver head coach at the start of the 1980s?

4. True or false – in 1985 the Broncos had an 11-5 season but still missed out on the playoffs?

5. During a wintry 1985 game at Mile High, which team was forced to try and throw a pass on a field goal attempt after a Broncos fan threw a snowball that hit the holder?

6. The Broncos were routed 31-7 by which divisional rival in the 1983 wild card game?

7. Despite posting a 13-3 record in 1984, the Broncos lost in the divisional round of the play offs to which team?

8. Denver had two leading rushers in the 1980s whose surname started with W. Can you name them?

9. True or false – the Broncos never had a losing season during the 1980s?

10. Who led the Broncos in receiving for five successive seasons from 1981 until 1985?

11. Which former Utah State defensive tackle posted 73.5 sacks in a nine-season career with the Broncos that stretched from 1980 until 1988?

12. The Broncos blew a 24-0 lead, eventually losing 30-27, against which team in 1988?

13. Which future head coach joined the Broncos coaching staff as receivers coach in 1983?

14. Which Broncos offensive lineman made the AFC Pro Bowl roster in 1986 and 1987?

15. Despite being taken with the 26th overall pick in the 1988 draft, which defensive tackle failed to play a single game for the Broncos?

16. Which barefoot kicker won a 478-player tryout to secure his place on the Denver roster?

17. Which running back led the Broncos in rushing in 1989 with 1,151 yards?

18. In 1984, the Broncos had a 1,000-yard rusher and a 1,000-yard receiver in the same season. Who were the two record-breaking players?

19. The Broncos were involved in just a single tie during the decade. Against which team did Denver share the spoils in 1987? a) Chicago b) Detroit c) Green Bay

20. With 191 appearances, who is the Broncos' most prolific defensive player? a) Tom Jackson b) Karl Mecklenburg c) Steve Atwater

Quiz 17: Answers
1. The Orange Crush 2. Floyd Little 3. Dallas Cowboys 4. Louisiana Superdome 5. Oakland Raiders 6. Rick Upchurch 7. Pittsburgh Steelers 8. Oakland Raiders 9. Red Miller 10. Rob Lytle 11. Norris Weese 12. Randy Gradishar 13. John Ralston 14. Charley Johnson 15. Jon Keyworth 16. Otis Armstrong 17. Haven Moses 18. Jim Turner 19. Pittsburgh 20. 1977

Quiz 19: 1990s

1. The Broncos' first overseas appearance was in London. Which Asian capital hosted their second?

2. In 1991 the Broncos lost the AFC Championship decider to which team?

3. With John Elway injured, which two rookie quarterbacks went in on a play-by-play basis during a four-game run during the 1992 season?

4. Who was the Broncos head coach during the 1993 and 1994 seasons?

5. Prior to taking the reins in Denver, Mike Shanahan had a brief spell in charge of which team?

6. In 1999 Shannon Sharpe became the Broncos' all-time leading receiver. Whose record did he break?

7. Four members of the Broncos Super Bowl XXXIII roster had a first name and surname that started with the same letter. Name the alliterative quartet.

8. The Broncos scored 28 unanswered first quarter points in a 1998 rout of which NFC team?

9. Who rushed for 1,159 yards in 1999, at that time the most rushing yards by a rookie Broncos running back?

10. Who started at right guard for the Broncos in Super Bowl XXXIII?

11. Which Bronco picked off two passes in Super Bowl XXXIII?

12. Terrell Davis tied whose NFL record after recording six successive 100 yard plus postseason games in 1997 and 1998?

13. Which Broncos defensive lineman added two Super Bowl rings to the college national championship he won with the Colorado Buffaloes?

14. The Broncos walloped which team 38-3 in the divisional round of the 1998 playoffs?

15. Which Broncos defender became only the second player in NFL history to win back-to-back Super Bowls with two different teams?

16. Which team did the Broncos defeat in the 1998 AFC Championship game?

17. What was Denver's record in the first season with Mike Shanahan as head coach?

18. Which Bronco set the record for the most all-purpose yards in a single game in a 1995 loss to the Seahawks?

19. Which Bronco did John Elway playfully call an idiot after diving for a touchdown in Super Bowl XXXIII? a) Terrell Davis b) Shannon Sharpe c) Mark Schlereth

20. Which team ended the Broncos' 18-game winning streak in December 1998? a) Dallas Cowboys b) New York Giants c) Philadelphia Eagles

Quiz 18: Answers
1. Dan Reeves 2. Cleveland Browns 3. Red Miller 4. True 5. San Francisco 6. Seattle (then in the AFC West) 7. Pittsburgh 8. Sammy Winder and Gerald Willhite 9. False 10. Steve Watson 11. Rulon Jones 12. LA Raiders 13. Mike Shanahan 14. Keith Bishop 15. Ted Gregory 16. Rich Karlis 17. Bobby Humphrey 18. Sammy Winder and Steve Watson 19. Green Bay 20. Tom Jackson

Quiz 20: 2000 and Beyond

1. Which team did the Broncos defeat in the 2013 AFC Championship Game?

2. Inspired by Tim Tebow, the Broncos rallied from a 15-0 deficit with just three minutes left to record an 18-15 overtime win over which team in 2011?

3. The Broncos beat which team 31-20 in their first ever game at Sports Authority Field at Mile High?

4. Which Broncos great suffered a broken leg in that historic opening game?

5. Which four Broncos caught at least 10 TD passes during the 2013 season?

6. The Broncos lost back-to-back Wild Card games in 2003 and 2004 to which team?

7. In 2004, who celebrated his first start at running back by rushing for 193 yards against Carolina?

8. Which Broncos offensive lineman was named first team All Pro in 2013?

9. Who won more games as a Broncos starting quarterback – Jay Cutler or Kyle Orton?

10. Who rushed for a career-best 227 yards against the Patriots in November 2013?

11. Four players started at QB during the 2003 season. Which four?

12. The Broncos beat which AFC West rival in the Divisional Round of the 2013 playoffs?

13. Against Atlanta in 2008, who became the first Bronco to start on both offense and defense?

14. Who intercepted 10 passes during the 2006 regular season?

15. Which WR caught nine passes for 146 yards and a TD on his NFL debut against Oakland in 2008?

16. The Broncos won their first six games of the 2009 under the stewardship of which head coach?

17. True or false - the Broncos had a points differential of plus 207 during their record breaking 2013 season?

18. In 2003, the Broncos became the first team in NFL history to have two different players return a punt for a TD in successive games. Who were the two returners?

19. What was the fewest number of points the Broncos scored in a game during their record-breaking 2013 regular season? a) 10 b) 20 c) 30

20. The Broncos won their last ever game at Mile High Stadium 38-9. Which NFC rival did they beat? a) Arizona b) San Francisco c) Seattle

Quiz 19: Answers
1. Tokyo 2. Buffalo Bills 3. Tommy Maddox and Shawn Moore 4. Wade Phillips 5. The Raiders 6. Lionel Taylor 7. Shannon Sharpe, Harald Hasselbach, David Diaz-Infante, Bubby Brister 8. Philadelphia 9. Olandis Gary 10. Dan Neil 11. Darrien Gordon 12. John Riggins 13. Alfred Williams 14. Miami Dolphins 15. Bill Romanowski 16. New York Jets 17. 8-8 18. Glyn Milburn 19. Mark Schlereth 20. New York Giants

Quiz 21: Pot Luck

1. Which former Broncos head coach was named the team's defensive coordinator in 2015?

2. Linebacker Von Miller attended which college?

3. Which defensive back did the Broncos select with their first pick in the 2014 draft?

4. In one of the biggest shocks in playoff history, the Broncos lost 23-24 at home to which team in the divisional round in the 1996 season?

5. Which former NFL wide receiver is the commentator on Broncos games on radio station 850KOA?

6. Which former Bronco played detective Roc Hooper in the TV show 'Guiding Light'?

7. What is the name of the stadium at which the Broncos played their first overseas game?

8. Which Bronco DB returned a fumble for a TD in the final seconds of a crazy regular season clash against Kansas City in September 2015?

9. Which running back, drafted in the second round, was cut from the team in 2015 after just two seasons in Denver?

10. Jason Elam and John Elway top the list of most games played for the Broncos. Who comes next?

11. Up to the start of the 2015 season, the Broncos had been beaten in the playoffs three times by which two AFC teams?

12. Which member of the Broncos' 1997 Super Bowl roster is married to

former 'Baywatch' star and Playboy model Brande Roderick?

13. Which former Bronco was awarded the Pete Rozelle Radio-Television Award by the Pro Football Hall of Fame in 2015?

14. Which Broncos defensive tackle was voted to his one and only Pro Bowl in 1989?

15. The Broncos overturned a 24-0 deficit and scored 35 unanswered points to defeat which AFC rival in October 2012?

16. Which ESPN journalist and influential Tweeter was a Broncos beat reporter in the 1990s?

17. Which quarterback led the Broncos to the 1998 AFC Championship game?

18. Prior to Ryan Clady, the Broncos last used a first round pick on an offensive lineman to select which Georgia tackle?

19. Who holds the record for the most TD catches by a Broncos tight end in a single season? a) Clarence Kay b) Shannon Sharpe c) Julius Thomas

20. In the opening four matches of the 2013 season, the Broncos scored how many points? a) 159 b) 169 c) 179

Quiz 20: Answers
1. New England 2. Miami Dolphins 3. New York Giants 4. Ed McCaffrey 5. Demaryius Thomas, Eric Decker, Wes Welker and Julius Thomas 6. Indianapolis Colts 7. Reuben Droughns 8. Louis Vasquez 9. Jay Cutler 10. Knowshon Moreno 11. Jake Plummer, Steve Beuerlein, Danny Kanell, Jarious Jackson 12. San Diego 13. Spencer Larsen 14. Champ Bailey 15. Eddie Royal 16. Josh McDaniels 17. True 18. Rod Smith and Deltha O'Neal 19. b) 20 20. San Francisco

Quiz 22: The Numbers Game

What number jersey was worn by the players listed below?

1. David Bruton Jr, Steve Sewell, Mike Bell

2. Gary Kubiak, Kyle Orton, Tommy Maddox

3. Steve Atwater, Knowshon Moreno, Darrent Williams

4. Darian Stewart, Tatum Bell, Clinton Portis

5. Alfred Williams, Robert Ayers, Ebenezer Ekuban

6. Allen Aldridge, Keith Brooking, Tom Jackson

7. Mark Jackson, Rod Smith, Julius Thomas

8. Brian Dawkins, Charlie Greer, Louis Wright

9. Tom Nalen, Lonie Paxton, Manny Ramirez

10. Brandon Marshall, Tim Tebow, Jim Turner

11. Chris Harris Jr, Haven Moses, Lendale White

12. Shaun Phillips, Antonio Smith, Neil Smith

13. Omar Bolden, John Lynch, Gerald Willhite

14. Simon Fletcher, Max Garcia, Chris Kuper

15. C.J. Anderson, Olandis Gary, Peyton Hillis

16. Goose Gonsoulin, Sammy Winder, Willie Middlebrooks

17. Paul Ernster, Rich Karlis, Trevor Siemian

18. Keith Burns, Nate Irving, Al Wilson

19. Mike Anderson, Montee Ball, Reggie Rivers

20. Brandon Lloyd, Jacob Tamme, Shannon Sharpe

Quiz 21: Answers

1. Wade Phillips 2. Texas A&M 3. Bradley Roby 4. Jacksonville Jaguars 5. Dave Logan 6. Mark Schlereth 7. Wembley Stadium 8. Bradley Roby 9. Montee Ball 10. Tom Nalen 11. Pittsburgh and Indianapolis 12. Glenn Cadrez 13. Tom Jackson 14. Greg Kragen 15. San Diego Chargers 16. Adam Schefter 17. Jake Plummer 18. George Foster 19. c) Julius Thomas 20. c) 179

Quiz 23: Pot Luck

1. Gary Kubiak enjoyed his first regular season victory as Denver head coach against which AFC rival?

2. 'Lou-dini' was the nickname of which Broncos defensive back?

3. Which former Broncos defensive coordinator was the head coach of the Raiders between 2012 and 2014?

4. Up to the start of the 2015 season, which team had the Broncos beaten in the playoffs the most times in franchise history?

5. Which Broncos quarterback enjoyed a win-loss record of 39-15 in his four years in Denver?

6. True or false – Terrell Davis is the only player in NFL history to have run for 2,000 yards in a season as well as winning league and Super Bowl MVP awards?

7. Which reliable Broncos stalwart was the lowest rated player in the 2013 edition of the Madden Football video game?

8. Which back-up quarterback substituted for the injured John Elway during the 1998 regular season, winning all four of his starts?

9. Which Bronco holds the record for the longest touchdown run in franchise history – an 82-yard effort against the Raiders in 1962?

10. Fill in the blank – Reeves, ?????, Shanahan, McDaniels

11. In 2009, the last player from Denver's Super Bowl winning teams announced his retirement. Which player was it?

12. True or false – Ed McCaffrey was never voted to the Pro Bowl?

13. Which head coach refused to shake Josh McDaniels' hand after the Broncos thrashed the Chiefs 49-29 in 2010?

14. True or false – the Broncos lost 19 of their first 20 games against the Kansas City Chiefs franchise?

15. Denver overturned a 24-point deficit in September 1979 to beat which team?

16. The Broncos were routed 59-14 by which team in 2010?

17. Who are the three Broncos first round picks whose full name starts and ends with the same letter?

18. Who holds the record for the longest kick return in franchise history after 105-yard efforts against Cincinnati in 2012 and Philadelphia in 2013?

19. In 2013, the Broncos set a franchise record for scoring the most points in a game. How many? a) 51 b) 52 c) 53

20. Which NFC opponent was on the receiving end of that thrashing? a) Dallas b) Philadelphia c) San Francisco

Quiz 22: Answers

1. 30 2. 8 3. 27 4. 26 5. 91 6. 57 7. 80 8. 20 9. 66 10. 15 11. 25 12. 90 13. 47 14. 73 15. 22 16. 23 17. 3 18. 56 19. 38 20. 84

Quiz 24: Anagrams

Re-arrange the letters to make the name of a current or former Bronco:

1. He Only Jaw

2. Rill Venom

3. Starve Wet Tea

4. Jams Alone

5. Hid Storm

6. No Lament

7. Idler Travels

8. Mourn Toe

9. Born Extra Tony

10. Gin Nonpayment

11. Evil Evil Drums

12. Contort Quilt Bit

13. Hi My Capable

14. Don Ran Brash Mall

15. Hi Growl Suit

16. Elk Crank Grumble

17. Orphan Sans Hen

18. Numerals Same End

19. Memos Hi Saturday

20. A Swarmed Cure

Quiz 23: Answers

1. Baltimore Ravens 2. Louis Wright 3. Dennis Allen 4. Pittsburgh 5. Jake Plummer 6. True 7. Aaron Brewer 8. Bubby Brister 9. Gene Mingo 10. Phillips 11. Tom Nalen 12. False – he made it in 1998 13. Todd Haley 14. True 15. Seattle Seahawks 16. Oakland Raiders 17. Randy Gradishar, Kelvin Clark and Sylvester Williams 18. Trindon Holliday 19. b) 52 20. c) Philadelphia

Quiz 25: Pot Luck

1. Who are the two former Broncos head coaches who have also led another team to the Super Bowl?

2. Which city hosted Super Bowl XXXIII?

3. True or false - Shannon Sharpe made a cameo appearance in animated TV comedy 'American Dad'?

4. The Broncos scored 31 points in the fourth quarter of a 2013 game against which team?

5. @SonofBum is the Twitter handle of which Broncos coach?

6. 'The Snake' was the nickname of which elusive Broncos quarterback?

7. Which running back scampered 72 yards for a touchdown against the Vikings in October 2015?

8. Which former Denver defensive stalwart from the 1990s was nicknamed 'Chicken'?

9. Which much traveled wide receiver made his only Pro Bowl appearance while with the Broncos in 2010?

10. How many play off games did the Broncos win with Mike Shanahan as head coach after their Super Bowl XXXIII triumph?

11. Up to the start of the 2015 season, the Broncos had a 100 percent play off record against which five AFC rivals?

12. True or false – former Bronco great Louis Wright is now a schoolteacher in Aurora, Colorado?

13. Which Broncos full back made his only appearance in the Pro Bowl

in 1999 as a special teams player?

14. Which Bronco led the NFL in interceptions in 1996 with nine?

15. 'Blitz' was the title of the 1988 autobiography of which Broncos great?

16. John Olszewski is the only player in Broncos history to wear which jersey number?

17. 'House' was the nickname of which former Broncos tight end?

18. Which defensive player was on four losing Super Bowl teams with Buffalo but won two Championships with the Broncos?

19. How many play off games did the Broncos win between 1999 and 2011? a) one b) two c) three

20. In what year were the Broncos last shut out by the Raiders? a) 1972 b) 1982 c) 1992

Quiz 24: Answers

1. John Elway 2. Von Miller 3. Steve Atwater 4. Jason Elam 5. Rod Smith 6. Tom Nalen 7. Terrell Davis 8. Tom Rouen 9. Tyrone Braxton 10. Peyton Manning 11. Elvis Dumervil 12. Britton Colquitt 13. Champ Bailey 14. Brandon Marshall 15. Louis Wright 16. Karl Mecklenburg 17. Shannon Sharpe 18. Emmanuel Sanders 19. Demaryius Thomas 20. DeMarcus Ware

47328792R00034

Made in the USA
San Bernardino, CA
27 March 2017